THE CROWN OF CREATION

other books by the author

POETRY
Dawn Visions
Burnt Heart/Ode to the War Dead
This Body of Black Light Gone Through the Diamond
The Desert is the Only Way Out
The Chronicles of Akhira
The Blind Beekeeper
Mars & Beyond
Laughing Buddha Weeping Sufi
Salt Prayers
Ramadan Sonnets
Psalms for the Brokenhearted
I Imagine a Lion
Coattails of the Saint
Abdallah Jones and the Disappearing-Dust Caper
Love is a Letter Burning in a High Wind
The Flame of Transformation Turns to Light
Underwater Galaxies
The Music Space
Cooked Oranges
Through Rose Colored Glasses
Like When You Wave at a Train and the Train Hoots Back at You
In the Realm of Neither
The Fire Eater's Lunchbreak
Millennial Prognostications
You Open a Door and it's a Starry Night
Where Death Goes
Shaking the Quicksilver Pool
The Perfect Orchestra
Sparrow on the Prophet's Tomb
A Maddening Disregard for the Passage of Time
Stretched Out on Amethysts
Invention of the Wheel
Sparks Off the Main Strike
Chants for the Beauty Feast
In Constant Incandescence
Holiday from the Perfect Crime
The Caged Bear Spies the Angel
Blood Songs
Ala-udeen & The Magic Lamp
The Crown of Creation

THEATER / THE FLOATING LOTUS MAGIC OPERA COMPANY
The Walls Are Running Blood
Bliss Apocalypse

PROSE
Zen Rock Gardening
The Little Book of Zen

Zen Wisdom

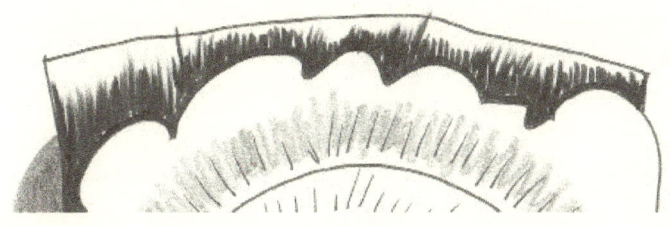

THE CROWN OF CREATION

a poem
with drawings
by

DANIEL ABDAL-HAYY MOORE

1984

The Ecstatic Exchange
Philadelphia 2012

The Crown of Creation
Copyright © 2012 Daniel Abdal-Hayy Moore
All rights reserved.
Printed in the United States of America

For quotes any longer than those for critical articles and reviews, contact:
The Ecstatic Exchange,
6470 Morris Park Road, Philadelphia, PA 19151-2403
email: abdalhayy@danielmoorepoetry.com

First Edition
ISBN: 978-0-578-10919-0 (paper)
Published by *The Ecstatic Exchange*,
6470 Morris Park Road, Philadelphia, PA 19151-2403

Also available from The Ecstatic Exchange:
Knocking from Inside, poems by Tiel Aisha Ansari

Front cover and all drawings by the author, except on pages 87, 124, 125, and collage portions on pages 103 and 114

back cover photograph by Malika Moore

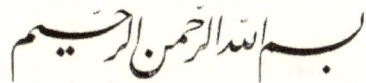

DEDICATION

To
Shaykh ibn al-Habib
(and the continuation of the Habibiyya)
Shaykh Bawa Muhaiyuddeen,
all shuyukh of instruction and ma'arifa,
to
Baji Tayyaba Khanum
of the unsounded depths

and for Michael McClure (1984)
and Salihah and Douglas Kirby (2012)

———

*The earth is not bereft
of Light*

CONTENTS
by first lines

AUTHOR'S PREFACE   8

1
Biological strata I love you they build up their...   13

2
That hairless homo sapiens...   22

3
Light strikes in the multi-veiled womb-chamber...   30

4
The message is sent. It is guided and...   38

5
Amoeba stage: inside the protective gelatinous envelope...   60

6
Fish-fin, spine, a fish is a spine swimming in water...   68

7
End of the 3rd week: 78

8
At 4 weeks: 82

9
At four weeks there is body, head, trunk and tail...   88

10
Have a look at the face!   102

11
What are all these glands in the body?   108

12
We are always the same body as that...   116

13
The embryo curled up in the womb...   118

AUTHOR'S PREFACE

This poem was suggested in a flash by a paragraph in Michael McClure's book, *"Scratching the Beat Surface,"* in which he quotes Ernst Haekel in the words used here as an epigraph, "Ontogeny recapitulates phylogeny." He goes on to say, in explanation, "Haekel meant that the individual, in his growth from meeting of sperm and ovum at conception, lives out, in fetus, the growth and evolution of his tribe; that first he is an amoeba, then a colonial organism, then an invertebrate, then a lancet, then a fish, until at last he is a mammal and a human."

Reading this brought together for me various strands of thought into one clear picture, in harmony with the cosmological picture of the Muslim saints: *"Man is a little cosmos, the cosmos is a big man."* And the view that Allah created the entire creation as a setting, as it were, into which He placed man, the jewel, the perfect diamond, as the seal and culmination of this creation. In terms of evolutionary theory, in the Muslim view all the flora and fauna were "prepared" for the appearance of man, and he is creation's entire anthology.

But counter to at least the popular notion of evolutionary theory, man was created, as were all the rest of the aspects of the creation, by a series of Divine Commands, like angelic triggers of light, rather than the purely mechanical adaptations to necessity, as if nature had a will of its own and could choose the most expedient path out of an array of possibilities. The most ludicrous example of this trend of thinking appeared in a recent "serious" scientific journal, which said that man developed light colored palms of his hands, prevalent in all races no matter how dark-skinned, in order to reflect more of the early morning light, so as to get more work hours into the day!

(A reasonable if radical argument can be built against evolutionary theory in general, that it either was developed for, or at least conveniently could be seen to bolster, a productivity flow-chart for the Industrial Revolution and all its bitter aftermath, taking such a toll on the human spirit.)

The imagery of this poem is largely based on the pictorial essay on the human embryo, *"A Child is Born,"* by Lennart Nilsson, photographs taken under the electron microscope of the phases in our inter-uterine development hitherto unavailable to mankind, after two-hundred thousand or more years of human history. Additional to this collection of remarkable photographs is the book, *"Behold Man"* by the same photographer showing our internal and external bodily surfaces in an equally amazing way.

This theme also enabled me to bring in the work of a little known biologist of the 1930s who wrote in French, Helan Jaworski, who, with rigorous biological exactitude, and profound poetic vision, saw that indeed in form and function, man contains within him many if not all the animal species of the creation. His discoveries, both intuitive and mechanical, even before these electron-microscope photographs were possible, are astonishing to us today. These themes, then, combined with the cosmological picture from the Qur'an and prophetic teachings of Islam, form the structure of this poem.

I recently learned that a traditional Mauritanian scholar was shown a photograph of a human embryo, and he turned away, reciting the formula familiar to all Muslims, *"I seek refuge in Allah from the accursed Satan."* Rather than seeing this as a medieval reaction, this should be taken as a warning from someone in a balanced social and spiritual situation, based on knowledge that is eternal/useful rather than just this-world temporal/useful. Perhaps man was not meant to be seen in his embryo state in the placenta deep and hidden in the maternal womb, in the darkness of the body, but rather as a born being, a living organism, fully developed as a baby, growing, going through the whole cycle of life in a body vulnerable to sickness and destined to die. Perhaps also that these sharply defined, sharp-focused visions of the embryo, of ourselves, *in situ*, are further evidence that this age has been turned literally inside-out. And no one can truly say that it has benefitted the deepest spiritual core of mankind, who was a higher being, with clearer inner knowledge, in certain past ages and in certain geographical locations, where the nexus was more or less pure, than he is now, in inverse proportion, with all his crystal-clear and rational outer knowledge. The essence still eludes us.

The Hopis believe that when the earth was viewed as a whole living organism from a house in space by the elders, it signaled the end cycle of time. Whoever was alive and conscious at the time doesn't remember the enormous impact of the space photograph of the earth, gorgeous and somehow vulnerable, jewel-like and lonely in the dark? But the visions have been shown to us — earth and embryo... the veil has been lifted — and now we must make sense of them.

1984

(Additional Note, 2012)

Since writing the above preface, the assumed non-gender-specific term, "man," has had a beseiged usage, and I thought I might go through and change it to a more politically palatable term, such as "humankind." But it proved to be a bit cumbersome, so I beg your indulgence to let it stand for what it means, *all humankind,* male and female, mutually inclusive. I also noticed in going through the manuscript in 2012 with an eye toward making drawings for the poem, in honor of the birth of our daughter's first child, that I hadn't really followed a rational progression of the embryo at every stage in time. But this work is intended not as a scientific one but an evocative poem meant to trigger some associative connections rather than presenting the theme assembled in perfectly symmetrical scientific data. The drawings also are not always illustrative of the accompanying stanzas, but rather emotive companions of the overall vision.

This poem remained in a folder since its composition, around which time I read it in its entirety at a poetry reading given at the now defunct Earthling Bookshop in Santa Barbara, California, where we were living at the time. I think I probably stretched my audience's patience with this one, for one of the older poets, perhaps eager for his turn, came up to the podium and said something to the effect, with a touch of the sardonic, "Well, that was a very enlightening lecture..." Faced with the prospect of publishing the poem in a book of its own, I decided on the strategy of separating some of the stanzas to their own pages, and making as many drawings as seemed appropriate to extend the manuscript to book length. The result you have in your hands, with my hopes for its heartfelt usefulness, and petitioned blessings for its ring of truth.

The final rhymed section (13) was inspired by stanzas read in Nicholson's translation of Mevlana Rumi's *Masnavi.*

Ontogeny recapitulates phylogeny.
— Ernst Haekel

The eye with which I see God
is the very eye with which God sees me
— Meister Eckhart

1

Biological strata I love you they build up their
crud and scum of leaf mold, worm-hole,
layer after layer from forest sea-floor,
itch of shadow alongside of tropic tomato,
length and slither of that lithe and little
skittering thing that goes up the radium xylophone
of subterranean phyla, bit after bit, the slow
and shadowed rise, the ache and urge!

Dot and drop of ectoplasmic spittle and drip
of the living-most pool in a molecular mini-spa,
molecules lying in their sun-bathed nakedness
in heat's palatial crater, crease and fold
of ostrich eye-blink, snooze-bubbled alligator
in a froth of black mud that makes oil look like
     lilywhite sheen, so
          deep is that blackness!

There is ooze upon ooze here, there is
Name upon Name here of Allah in piled
letters laying out the
          whole telegraphic array of the
leveled and layered veneer,
one crystal-clear level lying on another
          sky-high,
through niches and slits of forest, rising
like ponderous elevators through
elephantine chambers of redwood voices echoing
magnesium mellophones, tone after tone of one
chord that is heard through it all, the
whole this-worldly air-show, high-rising suds of
splendorous lusciousness,

tiger-lily and splash of green orchid, light like
splatterings of tiny crystalline lakes of light
spilling out across a decline
        as the whole mess rises.

This goes up through levels from the actual seafloor
that like valleys at mountain-feet pitch their slow-motion
seasons, always nearly the same, because almost
always underwater, though the time-clock
can go backwards, and a flint or shard
show. But the bleach and bleat of
instantaneous mountain peak, leaf-over-leaf-work
of uncoiled green-show, chlorophyll and protocol
of biological courtesy that
social-climbs from deepest scum
up through the crud of crude furniture, that
asymmetrical assemblage of forest-chair and lawn-couch
upon which
    suddenly one spring-blast
our hairless homo sapiens
       reclines.

He opens his eyes out of all this
verbiage nightmare, disentangles vines and verbs
from this intricate high-wire, as a
spotlight of Allah's purpose for creating him
shines down on his luxurious forest-floor
and all creation below him
turns up upon him

its eyes.

When he stands up the whole universe
increases in size.

2

That hairless homo sapiens
is the father of our tribe
our very Lord Adam
made up of multifarious muds.

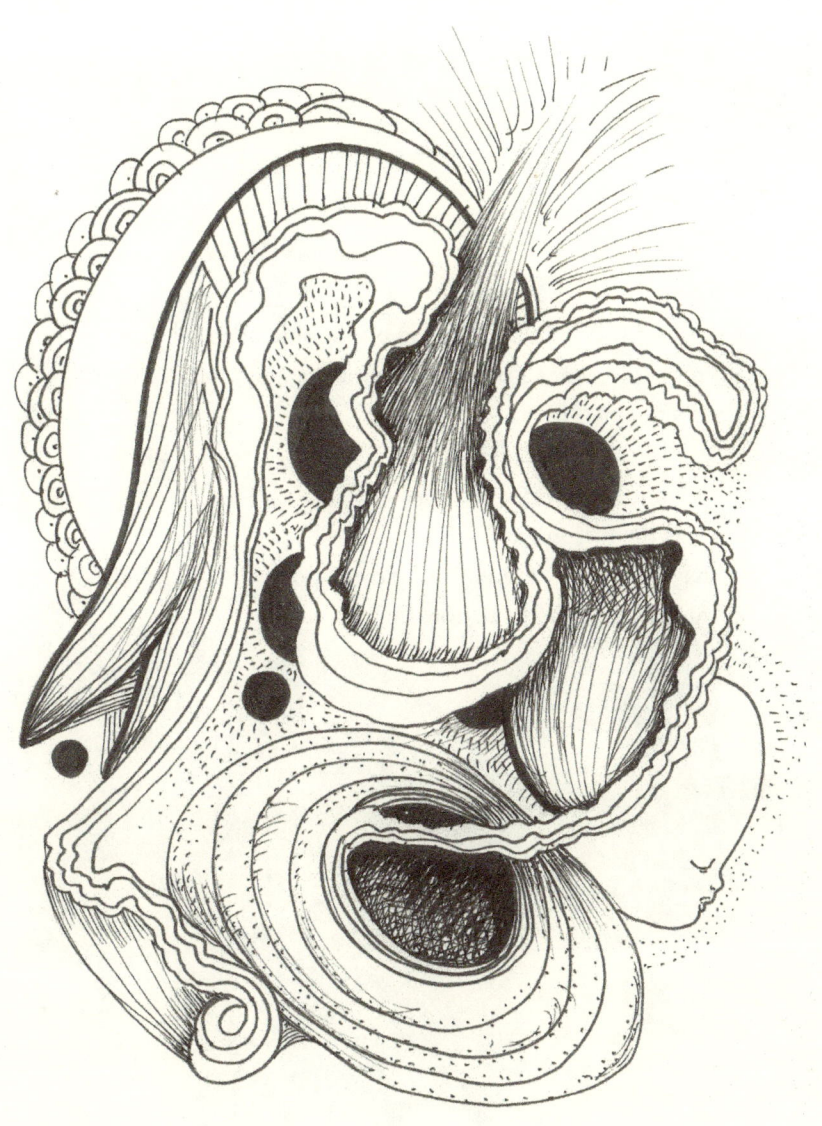

One mud like the sludge found on the side of an oil drum
or in the pit under a peat bog, very alive, and
deeply oozing.

    (Can it be that this mud we're from
       is the reason we
    have such an irrational and passionate
    mercantile love for petroleum?)

The other mud is of this and that color,
yellow from a yellow land, red from a
    red land, black from a black land,
tan from a tan, white from white,

and when they're mixed to a fine consistency
and ready for the casting
they make a potter's clay especially
    perfect for clear pinging,
a whistling clay, a

    porcelain.

All of this is the ingredients
    and we have come from that preparation
    in *potentia* in those loins of his

just awaiting the vibrant springing.

The continents were once one body, lying out under the stars.
They mixed their various landscapes
into one full-color photo —
   savanna and lush bog, prairie,
      volcanic dribble.

It stretched away in all directions in the first
        blush of innocence.
The dark under-loam, wormy, fetid and succulent,

the far fruits in sunlight
   dangling on their grammar of boughs.

The king of creation stood firm in the middle

and called out the names.

The echoes from that voice of his
still reflect on the canyon-walls of
whatever time there is left to us

so elegantly running out.

3

Light strikes in the multi-veiled womb-chamber,
    the inter-folded flutings of fluttering membrane,
a something flashes from nowhere not
made up of the provided components alone,
    a burst of KUN FA YAKUN: *BE!* — and it is!
        that blinds the darkness in there unknown to outsiders,

but is its own epiphany, its own glory to
flashbulb the event to the peak and tip of its
    glamorous destiny.

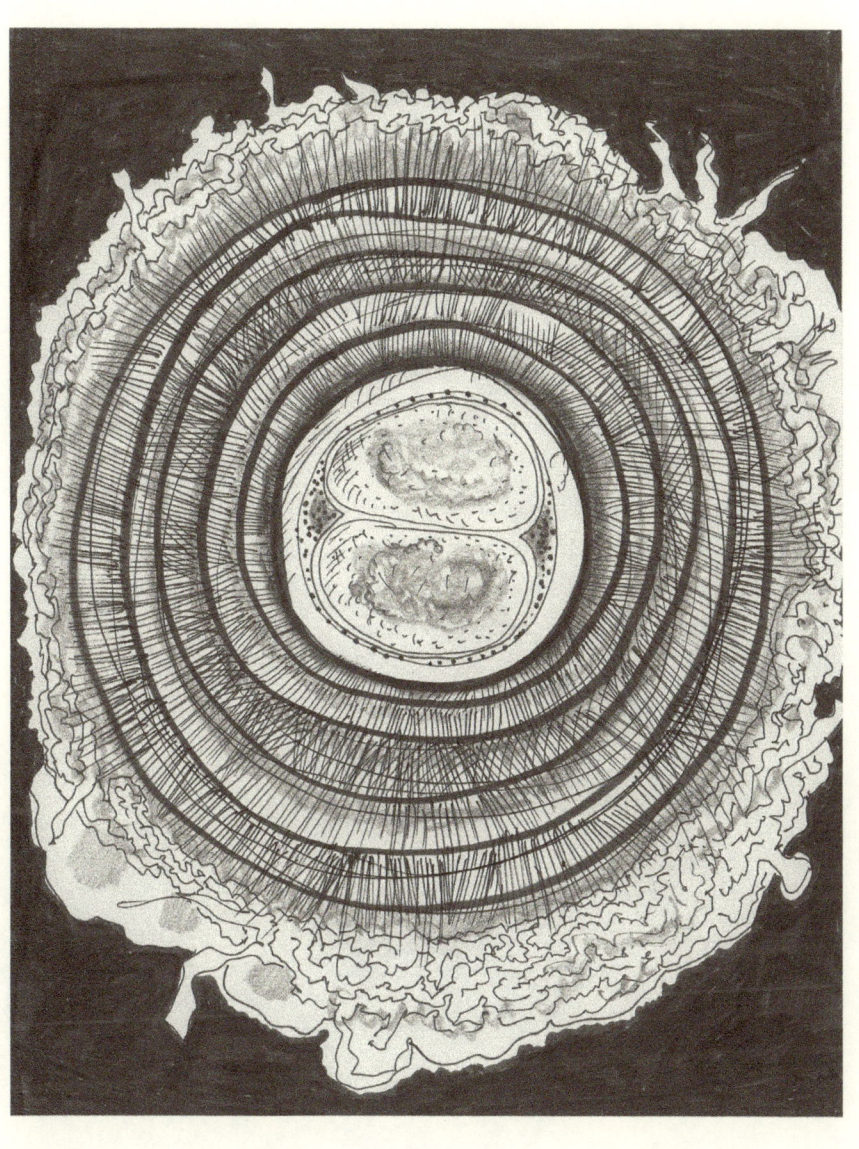

In the interior depths of the polyp
        moving in easy spurts
along ocean crags and cracks
        in deep sea water,

a mouth cavity opens around a
sudden something, just as here in the
modesty of the womb behind its
    intimate screens and venetian blinds

a life bursts into place.

A light above the sea
goes scudding into the distant
moonlight all across the
late-night waters,
    astounding the sailors
leaning over the rails with their
        beer-blurred binoculars.

*"Originally the sexes were virtually identical.
When living in the sea — as all living beings did
some hundred million years ago —*

*females as well as males could shed their sex cells
    in the surrounding water,
where fertilization took place.*

*Terrestrial beings are unable to do this.
However, the fusion of the sex cells, or fertilization,
must still take place in a medium similar to sea-water."*

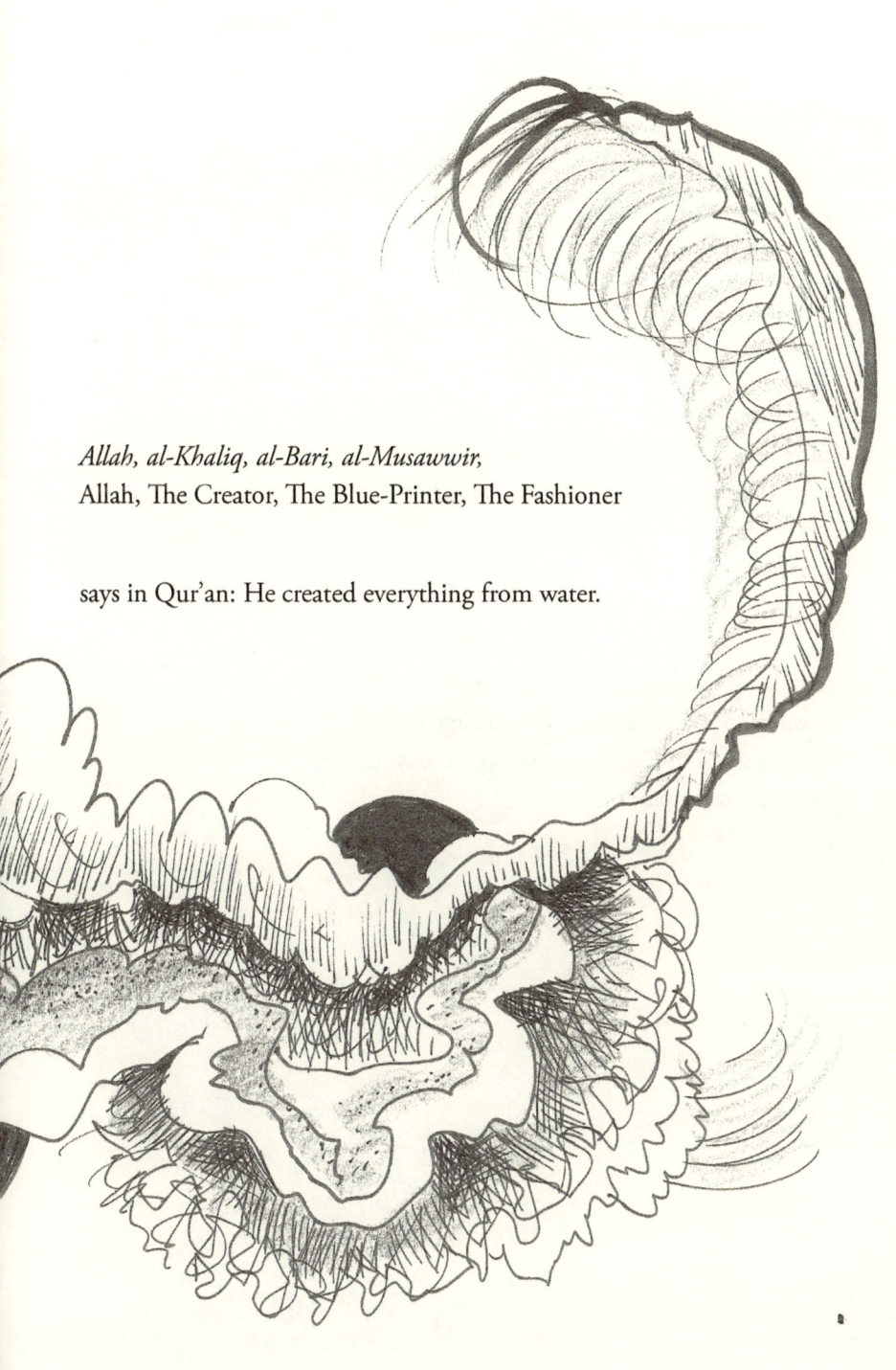

Allah, al-Khaliq, al-Bari, al-Musawwir,
Allah, The Creator, The Blue-Printer, The Fashioner

says in Qur'an: He created everything from water.

4

The message is sent. It is guided and
glided into place by no known hands
to ignite that confrontatory
   meeting, melding, merging and
sudden impactful splitting into

suddenly busy-as-bees cells doing all their
twenty-four hour activity of splitting and
taking sides and beginning to organize what will
soon become man.

It happens in sea-water. The uterus like a sea-polyp,
visually elongated, Fallopian tube like a

fluttering sea-lettuce, aurora borealis
        deep inside the female form,

fluttering its
        interstellar lights.

And the one ovum produced in the ovary
comes down dressed to kill descending the
    Fallopian staircase on her
way to the debutant's ball.

One a month. In a lifetime about 400 debutants in all,
    prima donnas each one of them,
most doomed to an early death,

but each one of them special.

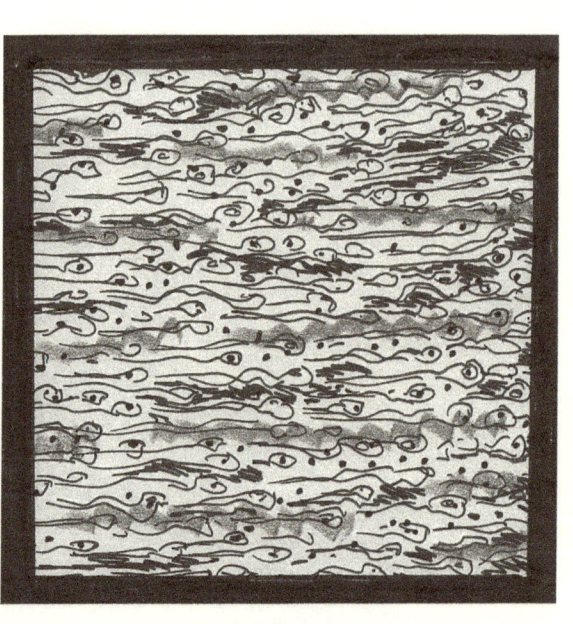

And the sperm, those tadpoles, like F. Scott Fitzgerald
       dandies, all slinky and snappy, come
slithering in on a jet-propelled up-thrust,
seeking out their dear darling in her
    shimmering screen. Her veils and
       coy aloofness, to fan her

face behind a
fluted wavering.

They swarm. Like drones. Like the termites on wings
       who mate in mid-air to fill the
  Nigerian jungle paths with petals
then fall to the ground
   still locked, to lope off to found
a conical termitary, those red
      towers built crazily,

these swains swim like mad for their
White Goddess shyly swimming —

*"It has been calculated that the number of
sperm equal to the present population of the earth
could easily fit in a thimble.*

*Six or seven good ejaculations would yield
      a sufficient number."*

The male produces billions all the time, from many
parts of his body, from the first cells of his body,
   since they contain
      the complete code.

Each man walking around with the entire
earth's population microscopically within him,
    image within image, shade
within shade. The entire population of China
bobbing in his body as on a junk.

Then Russia and Australia, India and all.

Then over a lifetime the whole galaxy, all the matter in it
multiplied, carried around inside a man

waiting for the message to get through.

The message. Getting through. Through thick
and thin. Up through the mucousy
		cervix whose film is thinned out for their
passage, and when they come to the
ovum they swarm like bees around a pollen-ball,

the bravest and most intrepid among them
by the explicit Decree of the Decreer,
digging its head into the membrane
like an ordinary tick.

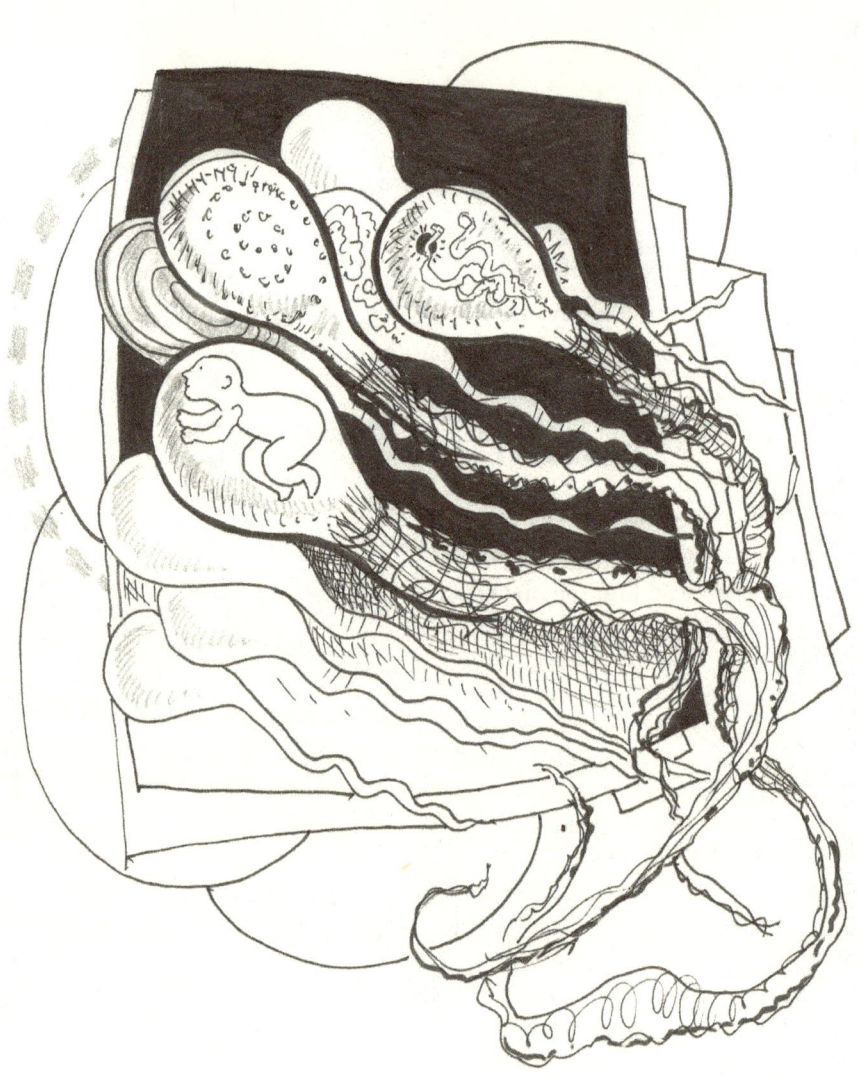

How many hopefuls die of heartbreak! Their various
headlights go out, and like expiring tadpoles
shrivel in the tide pool, their snapping
        whip-tails now slack.

"When the sperm is completely submerged in the ovum
it dissolves, and the genetic material
     is set free.
The genes of the future parents meet for the first time."

The amoeba is catapulted into
    immediate stardom.
        The gala event is set in motion
in the stage set by the womb.

Tables have been pushed aside, the crowd is hushed, the
    chromosomes meet. They pair off for the
neural dance.

X's and Y's are sorted out. The Morse Code
alphabet is brought to life.

The message is put into words. The intercoil
    interlaces, and the DNA xylophone plays its
scale, only certain of the
lettered chromosomes siding

with certain letters of the others, making the
    spiral staircase ascend
to carry the passengers home
into the upper regions of the library.

When Sayyedna 'Ali was asked of what life was composed
over 1400 years ago, he said, *"Two coils
          intertwined."*

The alphabet bed-springs are arranged, for
Allah says: *"We have created everything in pairs.*

*— O mankind, have fearful awareness of your Lord
Who created you from a single self,*

and created from it its mate,

*and from the two has spread abroad
many men and women."*

Deep inside this kaleidoscope
the amoeba multiplies its shrine.

The life-germ delicately plays back all the
   molecules ever living.

They burst in, by Allah, into how many separate
     channels,
tuned in to the central Transmitters

     to a fine hair-line.

The stars are out, we can see them
across the patchwork mileage of the skies.

All carousing in their passage
to the final body

opening its eyes,

Adam stands and praises his Creator, and glances at the Gate
and sees the words spelled out in Arabic that fulfill
   his earthly fate:

     La ilaha illa Allah
     Muhammad Rasulullah

The muds have been mixed, the clays congealed,
the galaxies swirling overhead. Mist sang.

The chromosomes meet in the deepest dark.

Allah said: *"Be!"* —

No god but Allah
Muhammad Prophet of Allah

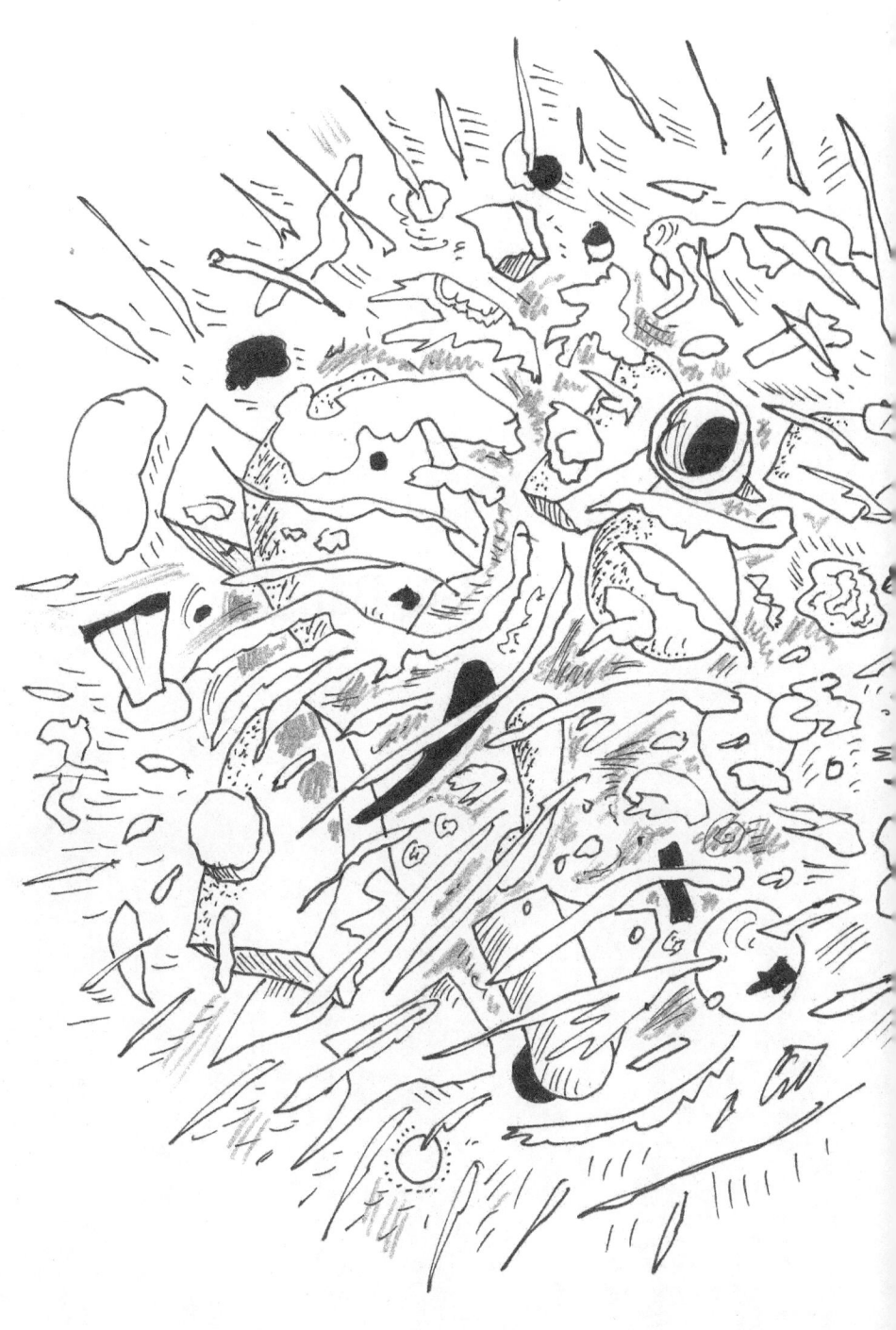

Big Bang!

5

Amoeba stage: inside the protective gelatinous envelope
the first polar body is "pinched off."

Twenty-four hours later, the fertilized ovum divides.
The first two cells come into existence.

Beehive, anthill, minnow-pool, China.
Organized work-loads for the carriers of the message,
    around the clock, themselves the actual
ticking clock like break-dancing jerking in
infinitesimal light-bursts of the overflowing river
    into place, each tattoo tip-tap of the

interstate message zooming the
    telephone line-wires to the
        action fulfilled.

So that the colony thrive! It jumps into place.
Life has invaded the place.

It's a jumping place.

All, individually pinching off and
    bubbling out, carrying
explicitly the coded
    instructions in His plan,

the secret blueprint projected for each
crystal or cell constructed, as they
    absolutely rigorously
        fall into place,

bursting out from the shadow-form in nothingness
        and scurrying to their place.

The place, the promontory, the blessed
one-time bit of geography, the stretching
sacred sands and tensile-strength valley-ways,
   the mountain-paths and peninsulas
under the sun.

Colonies thrive in the
craziest places, troglodytes
breathe underground.

Others build fortresses, great thickness against sandstorms,

others somehow survive in metropolises
       like Metropolitan New York,
   half underground.
Speeding to their meeting-places,
passengers in shuttering cars going
     past each other, subway riders behind newspapers,
         getting instructions for the

corporate mahogany tabletop elbow-jam
as they side-talk the issues to build a further
      colony in space.

Cells divide in the dark here,
ticking precise nick-jumps in time.

Phosphorous bubbles multiply on schedule
innocent of all crime.

6

Fish-fin, spine, a fish is a spine swimming in water.
The rush of the cascade waterfall
 doesn't disturb the blinkless
 fish in their afternoon pool.

Third week: embryo
with an obvious body and tail.
It looks like a luminous shrimp,
 more transparency than matter.

A film, a scant projection
 on the film of watery existence that meets it.

Blinkless it goes on, jerking in the amniotic water
 like a seahorse,
a flexible glass window onto a faceless positioning
 in the world.

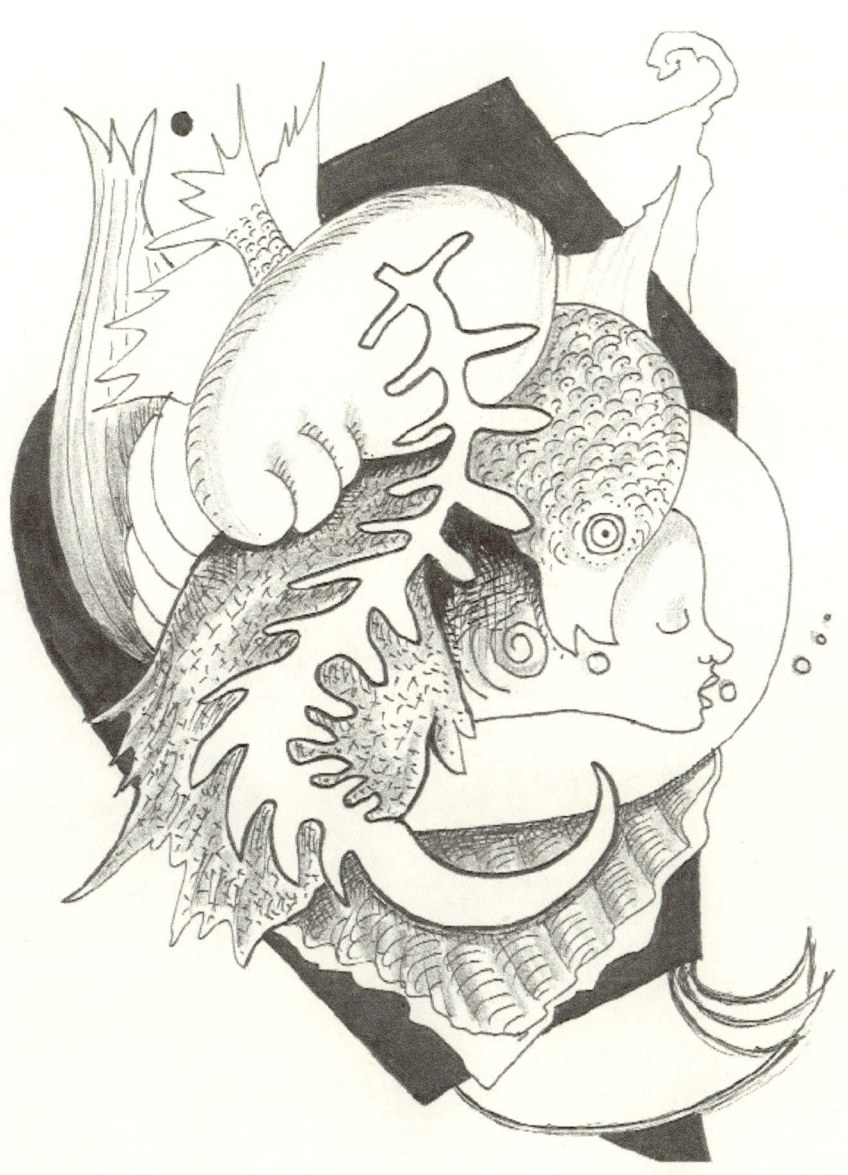

Silent? A light shines everywhere.
Dark? A hum of juices.
Endless. The shine of waterfalls cascades it
    with its embryonic foam

spilling out into space.

Like a chicken in the egg, it has a yolk sac right next to it manufacturing blood-cells for its build-up since

as yet no bloodstream exists.

It has a tail curling outward like a little lizard, it comes
    to a point.
More spine, though no spine has started yet,
more fish, though its destiny is man.

(The fisherman casts his elegant line,
   it scripts its calligraphy in space
      and lands in the mouth
of its willing victim
who cannot blink
   but saucer-eyed comes up

to lie on a pure white chinaware platter
that glides on a linen tablecloth like a cloud.)

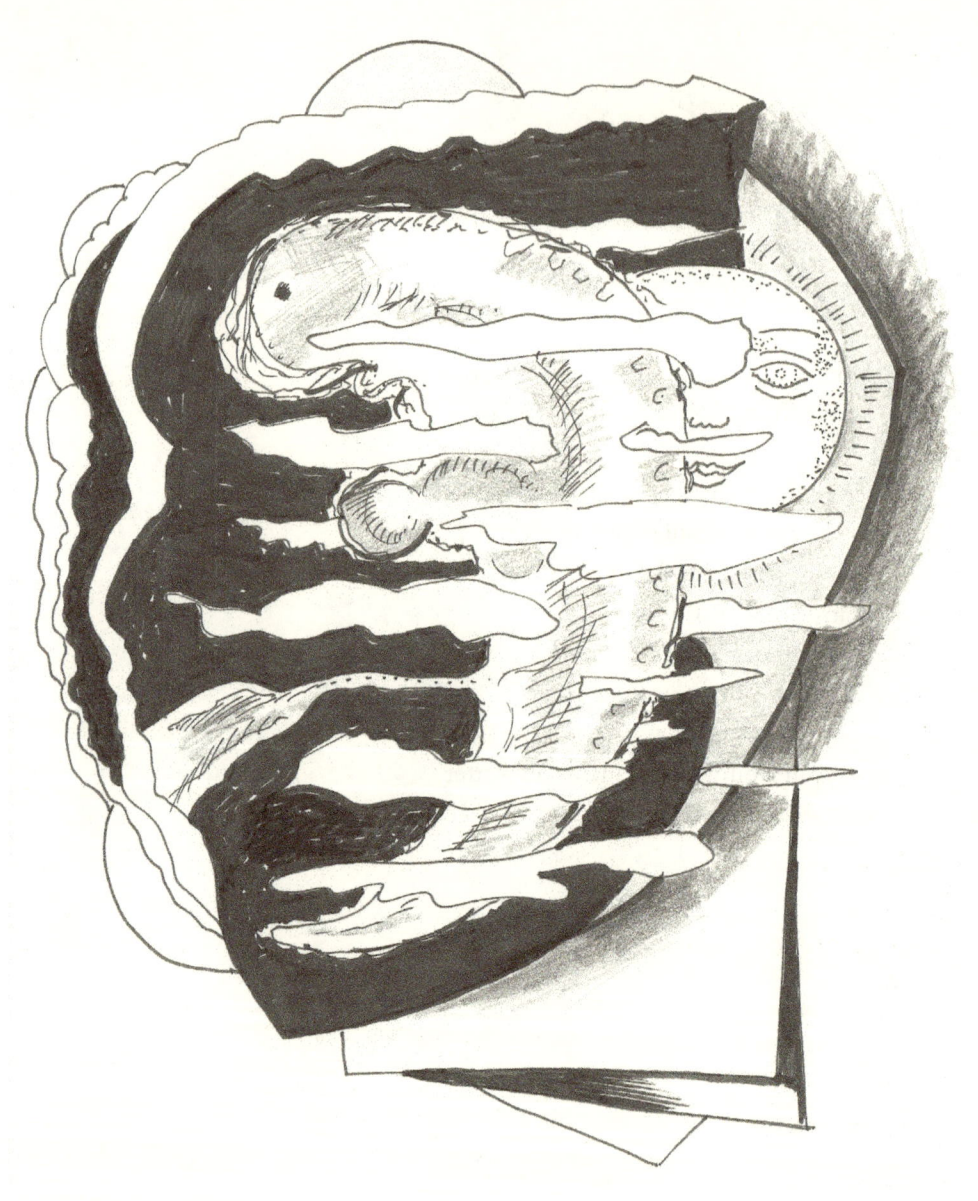

A future eye as yet looks on nothing.
The embryo body is the size of the crescent on a fingernail.

What will it be when it grows up to be?
For it definitely is, at this point, a something.

The whole phyla of existence passes through it.
The whole cosmological star-dust tear-duct
    presses its moisture out on the plan.

The vesicle has dug its way deep in the uterine lining.
Like a leech, it won't let go.
Like a barnacle, it has come to stay.
Like a cuckoo, it takes over the nest.
Like a hermit-crab, it moves into an empty shell.
Mistletoe growing on the topmost of the oak
    draws nourishment from its host
with the most refined kind of etiquette.

The embryo burrows into the lining of the uterus
and contentedly gyrates with a song running through its head.

The song is of sea whales, pterodactyls and logarithms.

The song is of deep sea tides
   on their way to the moon.

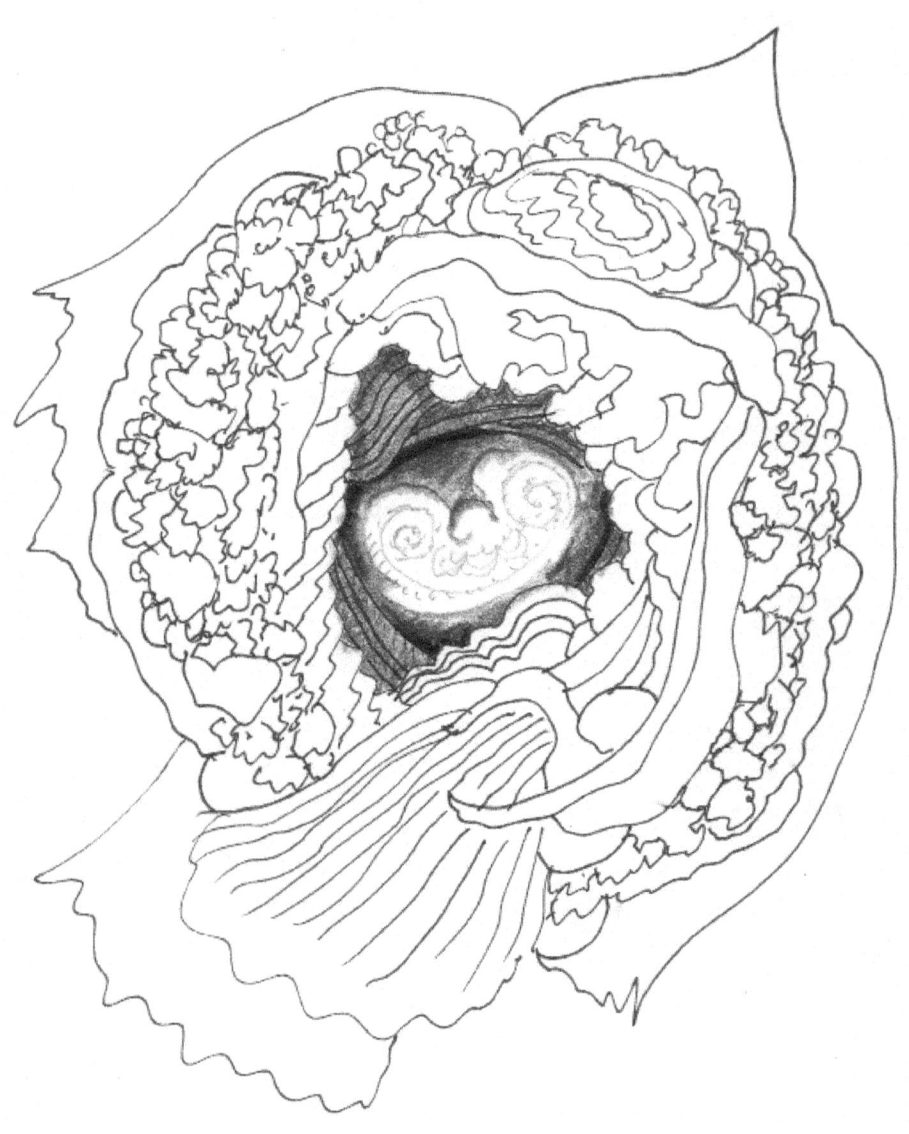

Jewels are strung out
    between the end and beginning of time.

At this point the fish-chicken heartbeat
    is becoming Hu-man.

Star debris floats through from
another millennium.

The secret of secrets is secure
in its virginal, inviolable shrine.

7

End of the 3rd week:
*"The outer germ layer — the 'skin' of the embryo —
thickens along a central line and
    simultaneously lifts into two
longitudinal folds.
This results in a groove leading from
       front to rear.*

*The groove closes to form a tube as the folds meet and fuse,
    beginning from the 'waist' and
continuing out toward the ends.*

*The top of the tube then swells to form a brain,
and nerve fibers begin to grow out from the
brain and the primitive spinal cord,"*

producing the rhapsody of miracle,

the haiku of miracle, the neon-curled

tube of miracle that spells out

the name of the as-yet unknown being who is

so curled up here, unfolding out from an

invisible center, moving out around in front and then so serenely

sealing itself together!

By whose command?

Only the blind, deaf and dumb
   dare fall down into
      ignorance.

Like trying to cover up reality with one hand.

8

At 4 weeks:

*"First, the anterior part of the brain sends out a hollow
stem to each side.*

The end of the stem expands to form a vesicle.

*When the vesicle approaches the surface of the skin,
it turns inward like a cup — fundus and retina
are established.*

*At the same time, instructions are forwarded to the skin:
'Make a lens!'*

*The skin then pinches off a bubble, which is placed in the
opening of the cup,
forming a lens.*

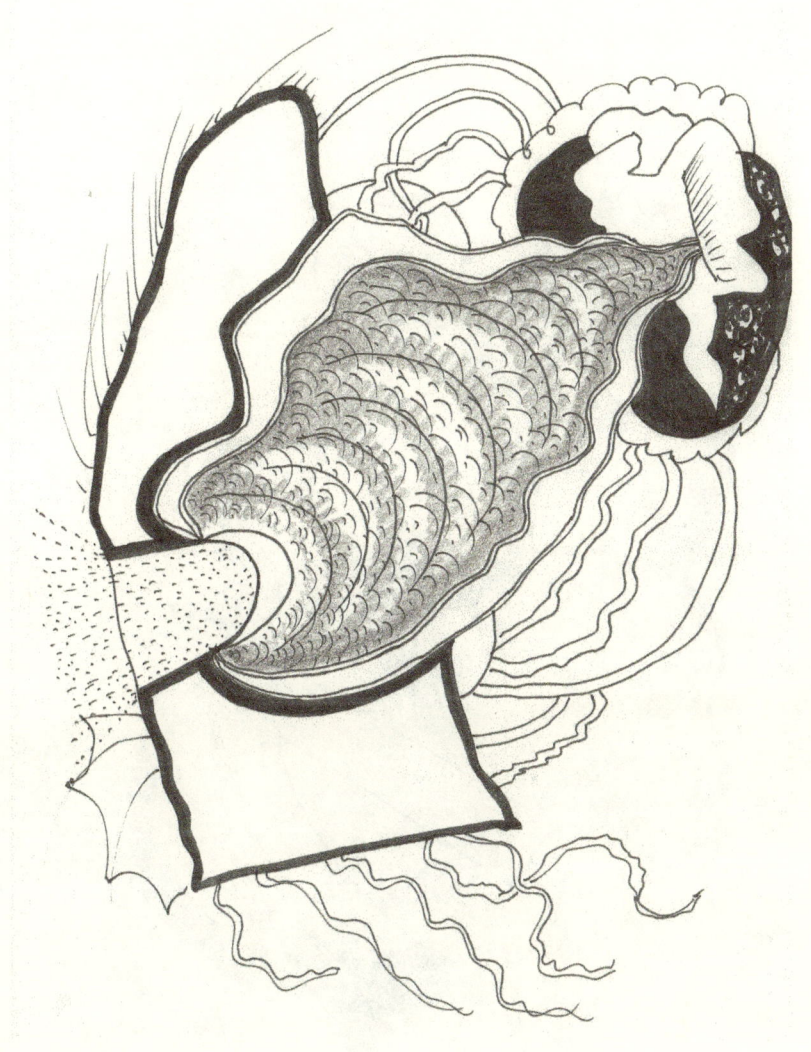

Then, *'Make a cornea!' And the skin covering the lens transforms itself into a thin, transparent cornea.*

On the front of the lens, the iris grows from the edges inward. Finally the surrounding skin is folded and forms two eyelids.

The eye is complete."

"To suppose the eye with all its inimitable contrivances to adjusting the focus to different distances, for admitting different amounts of light, and for the correction of spherical and chromatic aberration, could have been formed by natural selection, seems I freely confess, absurd in the highest degree."
— Charles Darwin
(*The Origin of the Species*)

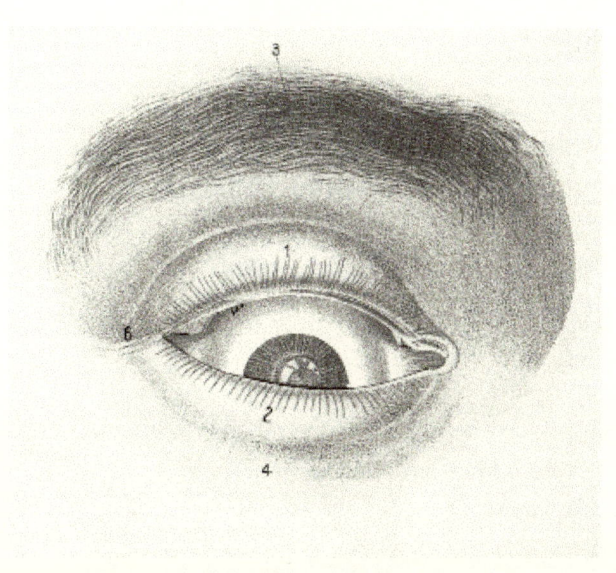

9

At four weeks there is body, head, trunk and tail.
The head bends down on crescent-curved neck
and the primitive mouth opens over the heart-throb.

Its heart is in its mouth. Its platypus paddles
    of arms and legs
        leaf out like stems.

Six gills form in common with fish and all vertebrates,
    but will form lower jaw, tongue-bone,
and vocable larynx.

The face of a snail with eyes at each side
    staring lidless and calm like a small
baby rabbit's.

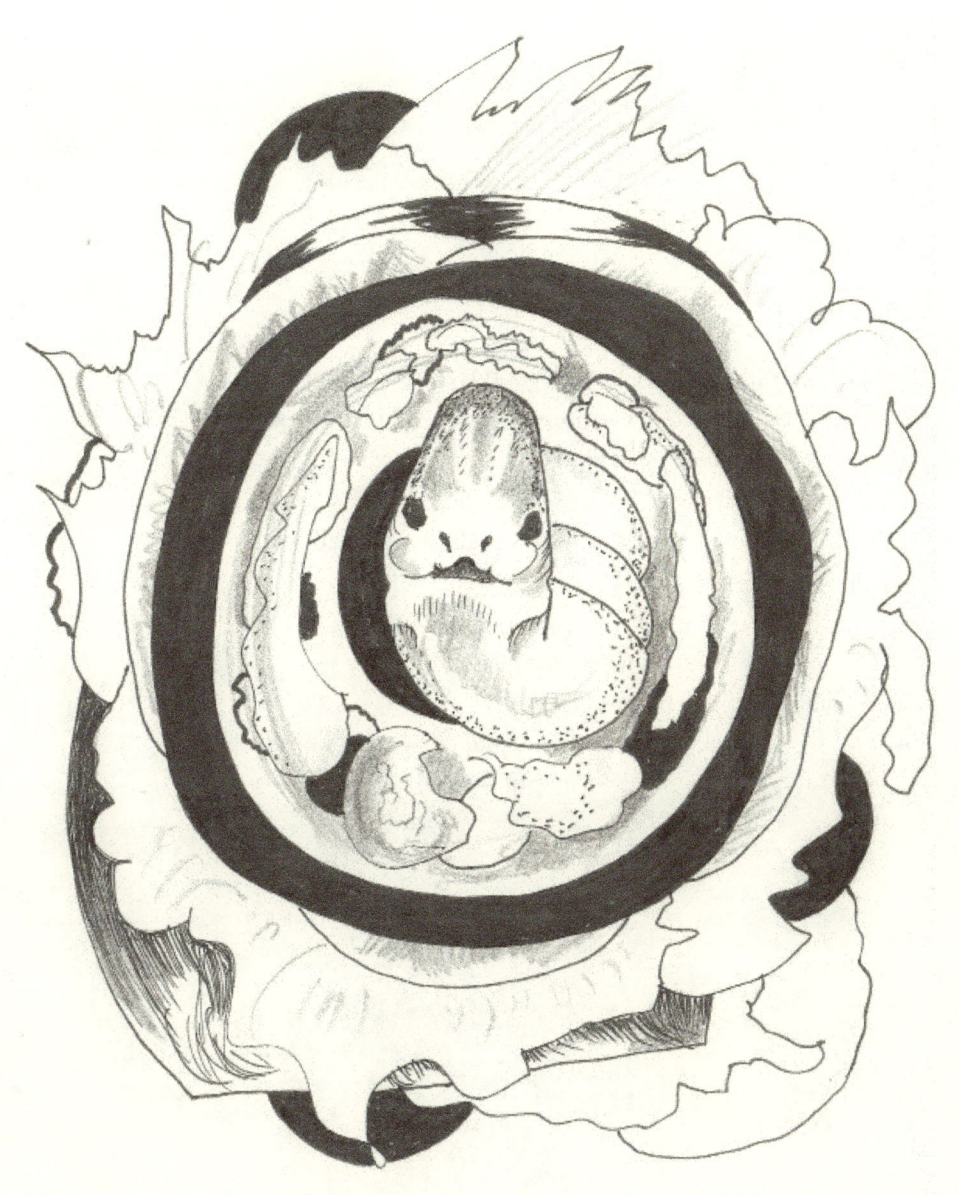

Three layers in the body form three different enfoldings,
the outer layer, or earth, making skin, hair, sweat-glands,
    brain and spinal cord.
The middle layer, or interspace, forms
    muscles, skeleton, blood-vessels, lymph glands
and a one-chambered heart
    that will differentiate soon into
        the multi-valved mosque with its
chambers and pillars
          through which the blood currents of knowledge
        burst in and flow out.

The third layer, or sky, is the intestinal tube.
Sponge-lungs will bud at the top,
urinary tract open out from below.

The little blood-sucker differentiates, the little mistletoe
thrives. The multiple branchings open out
    like efficient bee-hives.

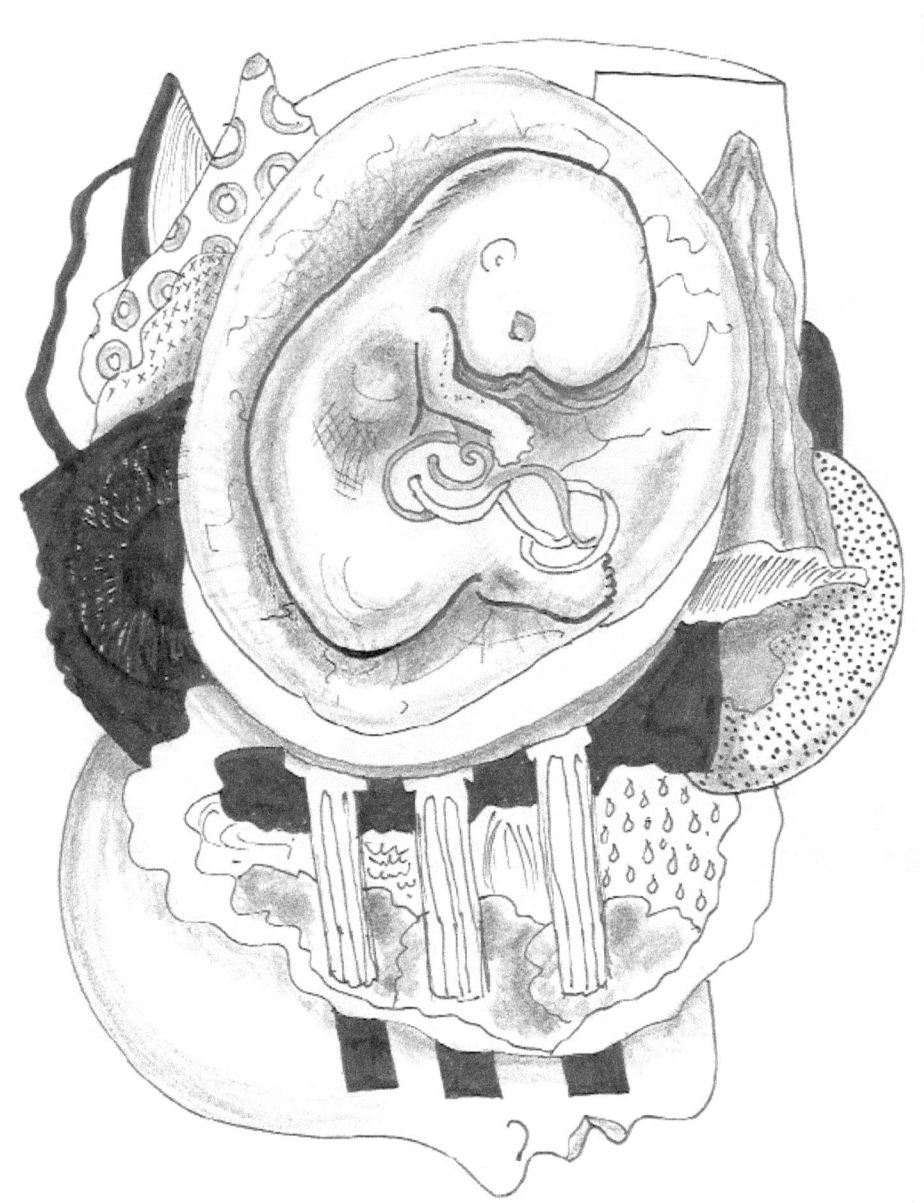

We develop from the head downward.

Fifth week: Brain stem grows so long it has to fold
    to find space.
Tail falls behind in its growth, and soon
    disappears inside the body contours.

The messages are computed and read out.

The multi-dimensional commands are enacted.

At each level of the Light
two halves curve around and fuse in the middle.

*"In the middle of the face, the forehead outgrowth
known as a process — the origin of the nose
and the middle part of the upper lip and upper jaw —
will meet and join the two upper-jaw processes,
which give rise to the cheeks and the
remaining part of the upper jaw and upper lip.*

*During the following weeks the nasal septum
will descend and join the two halves of the palate
which turn up like gates from either side of the
 primitive mouth cavity
and fuse in the middle.*

*This makes a 'two-story' arrangement:
the mouth-cavity with the palate as a ceiling,
and a two-room second-floor — the nostrils."*

*"Along the sides of the trunk, cells which will
give rise to the ribs are migrating in
            twelve streams."*

---

*"Moses struck the rock with his staff
and twelve streams gushed out
and every tribe knew its drinking place."*
                        (Qur'an: al-Baqarah 2:60)

---

*"They meet in the front,
in the center of the chest,
where a breastbone begins to form.*

Between the ribs, as well as in the body wall below the chest, future muscle cells are migrating."

The migration of human foot-print sandaled and barefoot,
millennial cellular seekers after water
round the bend of the sands as they
          sight the oasis.

Sugar-cubes draw ant-lines like breadlines in Poland.

The Hopi weave their snail swirl from
Mongolia around to Oraibi.

The whole outline of North and South American continents
scintillates from their temple-strewn trail
    to the Source.

*"Beginning from the back
and continuing out and around to the front."*

The foremost in unity
standing at the Gate with their call.

The Tribe of Adam

weaves historical webs

through it all.

10

Have a look at the face!

It could be anyone of us.

It could be all of us at once.

It could be the snarl-wrenched face of the mean

or the embryo-smooth face of the balanced.

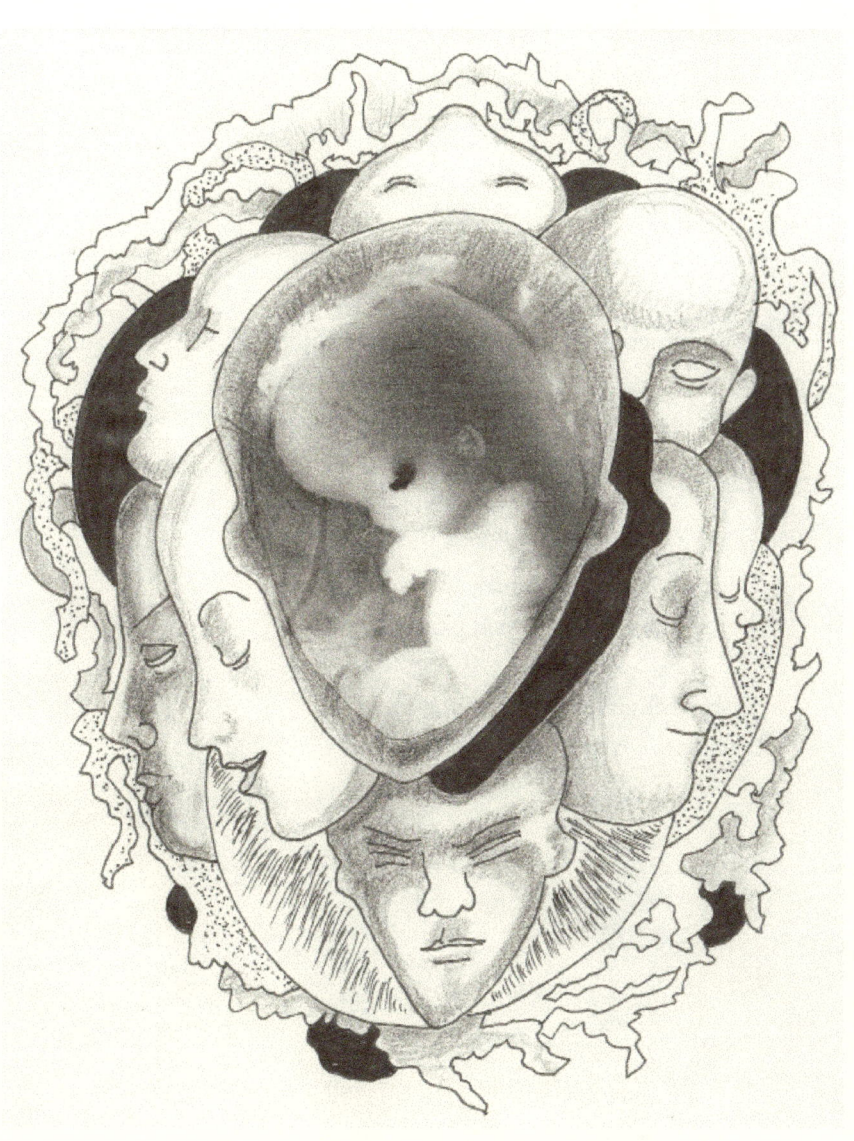

At six weeks the developing cerebral halves
are shimmering through the skin of the forehead.
Only the beginnings of a skeleton are found.
The spinal cord is shimmering through the skin,
    outlined by two delicately drawn red lines
        which are the two vertebral arteries.

This metropolis lives in the uterus which is
shaped like a down-turned papaya.

At six weeks it's no longer an embryo
but a fetus on its way to Allah.

Ibn Mas'ud said that the Messenger of Allah, peace and blessings of Allah be upon him, who spoke the truth and whose word was believed, told them the following:

"The constituents of one of you are collected for forty days in his mother's womb in the form of a drop, then they become a piece of congealed blood for a similar period, then they become a lump of flesh for a similar period. Then Allah sends to him an angel with four words who writes his actions, the period of his life, his provision, and whether he will be wretched or happy. After that He breathes the spirit into him.

By Him other than Whom there is no god, one of you will perform the actions of those who go to the Garden so that there will only be a cubit between him and it, then what is decreed will overcome him so that he will perform the actions of those who go to the Fire and will enter it; and one of you will perform the actions of those who go to the Fire so that there will be only a cubit between him and it, then what is decreed will overcome him so that he will perform the actions of those who go to the Garden and will enter it."

— Bukhari and Muslim transmitted it.

From this bunched-up incandescent shrimp in a bubble
to this striding, booming suddenly
    man or woman-about-town,

yelling and eating and just as suddenly
    going away!

This life just a few quick intimate hugs
then a going away —

and the going-away place

by far the longest!

11

What are all these glands in the body?
Endocrine, hypothalamus, pineal?

They are not gods in themselves.

They are like various microphones arranged for the Single Command.

What is this man?
His brain
(we develop from the head downward)

cut through is a tree, sliced
    the tree of life,
and we have grown dangling down from it,
roots in a dark earth.

And the tree of the furthest limit of matter, the
    Lote Tree at the edge, a spindly
        lacy almost immaterial shrub

beyond which no angel goes, but the Prophet
went on his journey to the Throne of Light!

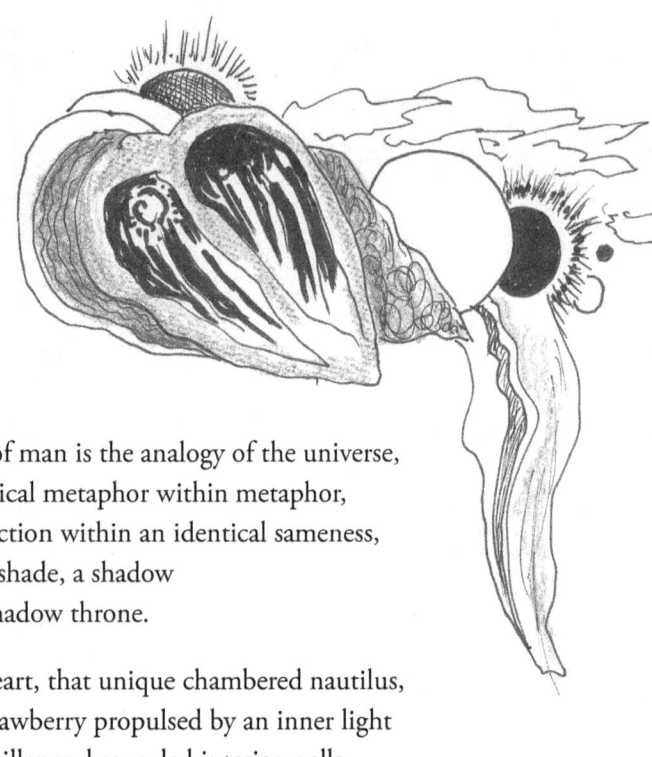

The analogy of man is the analogy of the universe,
intricate physical metaphor within metaphor,
form and function within an identical sameness,
shade within shade, a shadow
sitting on a shadow throne.

So that the heart, that unique chambered nautilus,
    enlarged strawberry propulsed by an inner light
with central pillar and rounded interior walls
    like a mud mosque in the Sudan,

the heart the size of our fists through which
in one lifetime 240 million liters are pumped
but through whose stained-glass walls in a sea of light
the antelope loves of a thousand origins leap
    on their way to their homeland

is not just the heart, but a heat, a melt of the
    molecular iceberg that surrounds us,

so that the bone-structure, lacy and hollow, a
Swiss-cheese manufacturing depot
tent-pole structure, stork-leg and timber,

so that the nerve-impulses, synapses, like spiders in
  form and function both, awaiting the tug
        that tells them a fly of sensation has fallen
    into the patient muscular web at last,

the spine like a fish, so that the spine like a fish
but upright, walking through air,

so that the gut like a snake, all inner-curled in
active hibernating sleep, moving in sluggish
inner propulsion, so that the

white blood cells like blob policemen who
cover the criminal element to remove it
sometimes perishing themselves in the attempt,

so that the lungs and respiratory system, like a
    bird who is all an apparatus for breathing,
and if we slice down the side of the head we have
the shape of a bird in our own interiors, from
    nasal passages to lungs which lie
inside like a pair of sea-rocks, coral
        inflating its Venetian lace,

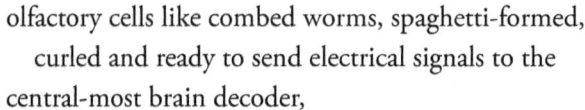

so that the tongue with its fungus forms,
    spongey and mushroomy, shelf-fungus
piled in ascending layers, so that the

olfactory cells like combed worms, spaghetti-formed,
    curled and ready to send electrical signals to the
central-most brain decoder,

so that the sense of touch, fingerprints
    like swirl-whirlpools, so

that the eye like a living being in itself, so
    intricately accurate, and then the brain
turns the perfect upside-down picture upright,

so that the hair like a forest-floor, the
    wavering limbs of flexible trees, scaly
calcium-shelled hair follicles, horny
    substance the same as fingernails,
plated like the backs of armadillos,
(and it is said that Adam had skin once that was
    covered with a hard plating like fingernails)

so that the entire body, once born, standing up
from original Adam at the gates of the
two creations, the Garden and the earth,

this sea we are, with the entire creation inside it,

this galaxy we are, our edges the edges of all,

this movement we are, going Gardenward or Fireward with
    assurance or wild trepidation,
one vessel of organic analogy, our
    tropical garden of actions

inside which the viewing spirit looks out and sees
itself each time!

As we go into ourselves, we see the world —
As we go out into the world, we see ourselves.

Mirror upon mirror at the great divide.

Multiple reflections ultimately unified.

12

We are always the same body as that
    stunted jellyfish with paddle arms and feet
        and snail face
that sits and stands and orates a few orations

then is planted, wrinkled and dry, underground,

hair oil for grass.

But this body is just a bud, a budding
    along the passage of the spirit through its
        dimensional levels, a

flowering garden of actions, this spirit
at its bodily intersections and salons,

making its honest or dishonest transactions as it
    speeds to the next sphere.

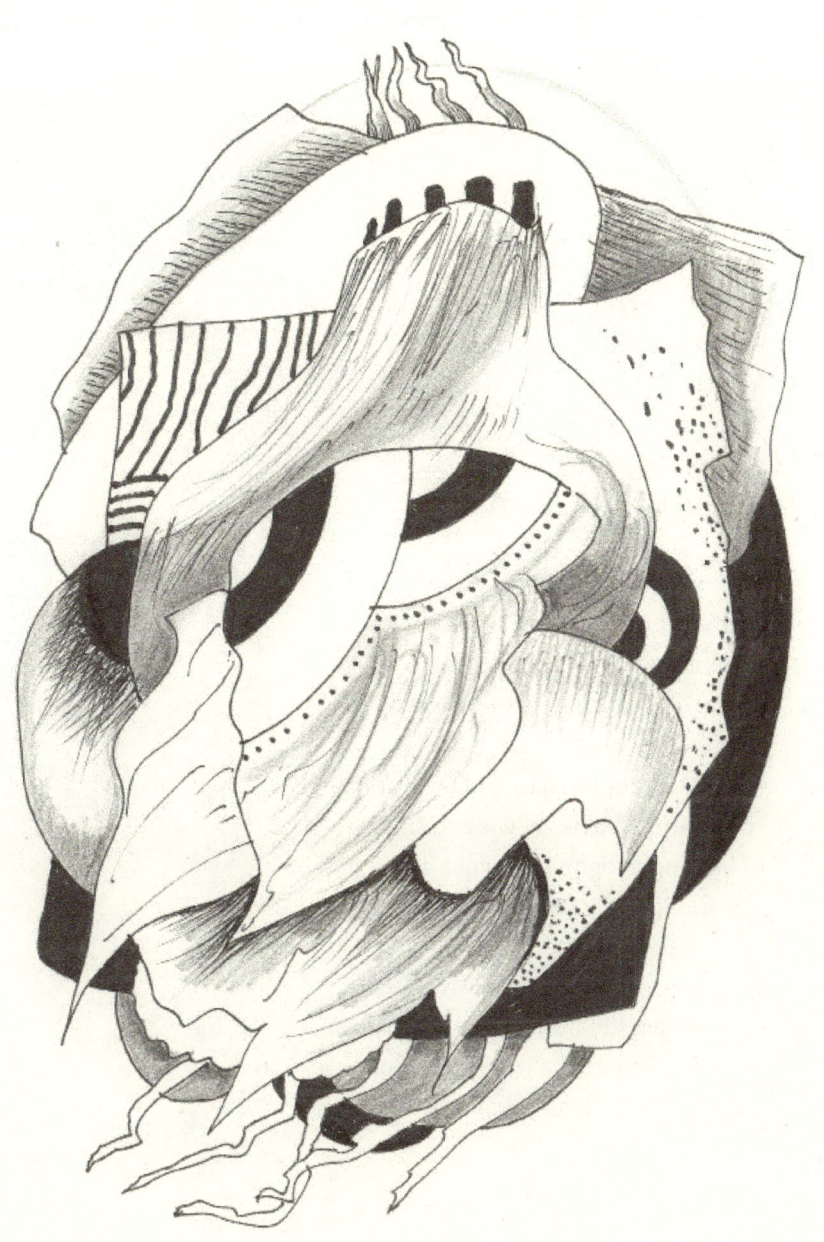

13

The embryo curled up in the womb
enjoys its comforts, furnished room,
hot, cold water, nourishing blood,
an even climate in fire or flood,
and feels no earthly inclination
to leave it for a higher station.

So when a kind voice comes to it
to draw it out through its only exit,
it stubbornly declines the offer
preferring the confines of its watery coffer.

"Come out of that narrow house of yours,
come out and bask on wide seashores
of light upon light as no light you've got.
A world lies here outspread past thought.

Out here a sun with its cheerful beams,
a moon that lies in the sky like dreams,
a sea that laps earth's wide green floor,
a sky of clouds, high hills and more

than can be described in a lifetime or two!"
"Please leave me alone," it answers. "This will do.
There's a sun and a moon in here as well,
and boom of tides and deepsea swell,

there's sky and earth and mountain heights,
flowers of spring and wintry sights.
As earth turns and digs up its cyclic seasons,
I'm quite content to not know the reasons
I should leave this space with its steam-heated walls.
Why should I wander through earthly halls?"

"But come out and see what you never saw
in the dark of the place you call light, and raw
is cooked here, life wide-spread with wings
that allow you to leap from molecular rings

of action to pure contemplation in one
leap that draws everything in under the sun.
But starlight circulates, rivers in space
coil galaxies out which the heavens enlace,

light travels faster than mind can scan,
but it's all in the human heart, caravan
of turning, constantly whirling spark
scouring cobwebs out of the dark!"

But the embryo deep in its couched contentment
stubbornly stays in its warm apartment
as long as it can, though at last must go
to see what exists that its wombworld can't know.

For this world's veil is equally thick fallen down
to keep us from seeing Allah's extravagant round
that we'll come to later but can taste here and now,
as a voice comes through these walls to show

a sun beyond our earth-sun's splendor,
a moonlight beyond the silver's tender
spray on any black lake that lies below,
a place where each thing is a chiseled rainbow

of prismatic delight, of voices and tales
beyond what we know here, this drama that trails
its bad dialog across floors of pain,
endless boredom of an endless rain,

a voice that beckons us out past the parameters
of a world too structured in its diameters
to a gesture that hovers like a balanced bough
and a word of the Next World's original flow.

"Come out of the narrow walls of your den,
anatomical straps and your fleshly pen
that writes endless contracts to suffocate breath
and lead a dull brain to the couch of death.

To hold the heart down from its condor's flight
that spreads black wings past the black of night
out through the walls of opinion too tight
to enter the dominion of endless light.

Another sun beams down in this sphere,
another moon is its dazzling mirror,
another song flings its high-pitched noise
of waterfall atmospheres held in a praise

so exalted no matter can be said to exist
and all is withdrawn into deep primal mist.
The mist of first love, the Creator's breath
blown out in true being.

                    The only path.

ABOUT THE AUTHOR

Born in 1940 in Oakland, California, Daniel Abdal-Hayy Moore had his first book of poems, *Dawn Visions*, published by Lawrence Ferlinghetti of City Lights Books, San Francisco, in 1964, and the second in 1972, *Burnt Heart/ Ode to the War Dead*. He created and directed *The Floating Lotus Magic Opera Company* in Berkeley, California in the late 60s, and presented two major productions, *The Walls Are Running Blood*, and *Bliss Apocalypse*. He became a Sufi Muslim in 1970, performed the Hajj in 1972, and lived and traveled throughout Morocco, Spain, Algeria and Nigeria, landing in California and publishing *The Desert is the Only Way Out*, and *Chronicles of Akhira* in the early 80s (Zilzal Press). Residing in Philadelphia since 1990, in 1996 he published *The Ramadan Sonnets* (Jusoor/City Lights), and in 2002, *The Blind Beekeeper* (Jusoor/Syracuse University Press). He has been poetry editor for *Seasons Journal* and *Islamica Magazine*, and the major editor for a number of books, including *The Burdah* of Shaykh Busiri, and *The Prayer of the Oppressed* of Imam Nasir al-Dar'i, translated by Shaykh Hamza Yusuf, and the poetry of Palestinian poet, Mahmoud Darwish, translated by Munir Akash, including *Adam of Two Edens, State of Siege*, from Jusoor/Syracuse University Press, and *Unfortunately it was Paradise*, from the University of California Press. He is also widely published on the worldwide web: *The American Muslim,* and his own blog: www.ecstaticxchange.wordpress.com, and his website: www.danielmoorepoetry.com, among others. He has twice been a winner of the Nazim Hikmet Poetry Prize, for 2011 and 2012. The Ecstatic Exchange Series is bringing out the extensive body of his works of poetry (the full list of the books in print on page 2).

POETIC WORKS by Daniel Abdal-Hayy Moore
Published and Unpublished

Dawn Visions (published by City Lights, 1964)
Burnt Heart/Ode to the War Dead (published by City Lights, 1972)
This Body of Black Light Gone Through the Diamond (printed by Fred Stone, Cambridge, Mass, 1965)
On The Streets at Night Alone (1965?)
All Hail the Surgical Lamp (1967)
States of Amazement (1970)

Abdallah Jones and the Disappearing-Dust Caper (published by The Ecstatic Exchange/Crescent Series, 2006)
Ala-udeen and the Magic Lamp (published by The Ecstatic Exchange/Crescent Series, 2011)
The Chronicles of Akhira (1981) (published by Zilzal Press with Typoglyphs by Karl Kempton, 1986) (published in Sparrow on the Prophet's Tomb, The Ecstatic Exchange, 2010)
Mouloud (1984) (A Zilzal Press chapbook, 1995) (published in Sparrow on the Prophet's Tomb, The Ecstatic Exchange, 2010)
The Crown of Creation (1984) (published by The Ecstatic Exchange, 2012)
The Look of the Lion (The Parabolas of Sight) (1984)
The Desert is the Only Way Out (completed 4/21/84) (Zilzal Press chapbook, 1985)
Atomic Dance (1984) (am here books, 1988)
Outlandish Tales (1984)
Awake as Never Before (12/26/84) (Zilzal Press chapbook, 1993)
Glorious Intervals (1/1/85) (Zilzal Press chapbook, ?)
Long Days on Earth/Book I (1/28 – 8/30/85)
Long Days on Earth/Book II (Hayy Ibn Yaqzan)
Long Days on Earth/Book III (1/22/86)
Long Days on Earth/Book IV (1986)
The Ramadan Sonnets (Long Days on Earth/Book V) (5/9 – 6/11/86) (published by Jusoor/City Lights Books, 1996) (republished as Ramadan Sonnets by The Ecstatic Exchange, 2005)
Long Days on Earth/Book VI (6-8/30/86)
Holograms (9/4/86 – 3/26/87)

History of the World (The Epic of Man's Survival) (4/7 – 6/18/87)
Exploratory Odes (6/25 – 10/18/87)
The Man at the End of the World (11/11 – 12/10/87)
The Perfect Orchestra (3/30 – 7/25/88) (published by The Ecstatic Exchange, 2009)
Fed from Underground Springs (7/30 – 11/23/88)
Ideas of the Heart (11/27/88 – 5/5/89)
New Poems (scattered poems, out of series, from 3/24 – 8/9/89)
Facing Mecca (5/16 – 11/11/89)
A Maddening Disregard for the Passage of Time (11/17/89 – 5/20/90)(published by The Ecstatic Exchange, 2009)
The Heart Falls in Love with Visions of Perfection (6/15/90 – 6/2/91)
Like When You Wave at a Train and the Train Hoots Back at You (Farid's Book) (6/11 – 7/26/91) (published by The Ecstatic Exchange, 2008)
Orpheus Meets Morpheus (8/1/91– 3/14/92)
The Puzzle (3/21/92 – 8/17/93) (published by The Ecstatic Exchange, 2011)
The Greater Vehicle (10/17/93 – 4/30/94)
A Hundred Little 3-D Pictures (5/14/94 – 9/11/95)
The Angel Broadcast (9/29 – 12/17/95)
Mecca/Medina Time-Warp (12/19/95 – 1/6/96) (published as a Zilzal Press chapbook, 1996) (Published in Sparrow on the Prophet's Tomb, The Ecstatic Exchange, 2010)
Miracle Songs for the Millennium (1/20 – 10/16/96)
The Blind Beekeeper (11/15/96 – 5/30/97) (published 2002 by Jusoor/Syracuse University Press)
Chants for the Beauty Feast (6/3 – 10/28/97) (published by The Ecstatic Exchange, 2011)
You Open a Door and it's a Starry Night (10/29/97 – 5/23/98) (published by The Ecstatic Exchange, 2009)
Salt Prayers (5/29 – 10/24/98) (published by The Ecstatic Exchange, 2005)
Some (10/25/98 – 4/25/99)
Flight to Egypt (5/1 – 5/16/99)
I Imagine a Lion (5/21 – 11/15/99) (published by The Ecstatic Exchange, 2006)
Millennial Prognostications (11/25/99 – 2/2/2000) (published by the Ecstatic Exchange, 2009)
Shaking the Quicksilver Pool (2/4 – 10/8/2000) (Published by The Ecstatic Exchange, 2009)
Blood Songs (10/9/2000 – 4/3/2001) (Published by The Ecstatic Exchange, 2012)

The Music Space (4/10 – 9/16/2001) (Published by The Ecstatic Exchange, 2007)
Where Death Goes (9/20/2001 – 5/1/2002) (Published by The Ecstatic Exchange, 2009)
The Flame of Transformation Turns to Light (99 Ghazals Written in English) (5/14 – 8/21/2002) (Published by The Ecstatic Exchange, 2007)
Through Rose-Colored Glasses (7/22/2002 – 1/15/2003) (Published by The Ecstatic Exchange, 2007)
Psalms for the Broken-Hearted (1/22 – 5/25/2003) (Published by The Ecstatic Exchange, 2006)
Hoopoe's Argument (5/27 – 9/18/03)
Love is a Letter Burning in a High Wind (9/21 – 11/6/2003) (Published by The Ecstatic Exchange, 2006)
Laughing Buddha/Weeping Sufi (11/7/2003 – 1/10/2004) (Published by The Ecstatic Exchange, 2005)
Mars and Beyond (1/20 – 3/29/2004) (Published by The Ecstatic Exchange, 2005)
Underwater Galaxies (4/5 – 7/21/2004) (Published by The Ecstatic Exchange, 2007)
Cooked Oranges (7/23/2004 – 1/24/2005 (Published by The Ecstatic Exchange, 2007)
Holiday from the Perfect Crime (1/25 – 6/11/2005) (published by The Ecstatic Exchange, 2011)
Stories Too Fiery to Sing Too Watery to Whisper (6/13 – 10/24/2005)
Coattails of the Saint (10/26/2005 – 5/10/2006) (Published by The Ecstatic Exchange, 2006)
In the Realm of Neither (5/14/2006 – 11/12/06) (Published by The Ecstatic Exchange, 2008)
Invention of the Wheel (11/13/06 – 6/10/07) (Published by The Ecstatic Exchange, 2010)
The Sound of Geese Over the House (6/15 – 11/4/07)
The Fire Eater's Lunchbreak (11/11/07 – 5/19/2008) (Published by The Ecstatic Exchange, 2008)
Sparks Off the Main Strike (5/24/2008 – 1/10/2009) (published by The Ecstatic Exchange, 2010)
Stretched Out on Amethysts (1/13 – 9/17/2009) (published by The Ecstatic Exchange, 2010)
The Throne Perpendicular to All that is Horizontal (9/18/09 – 1/25/10)
In Constant Incandescence (2/10 – 8/13/10) (published by The Ecstatic Exchange, 2011)

The Caged Bear Spies the Angel (8/30/10 –3/6/11)(published by The Ecstatic Exchange, 2011)
This Light Slants Upward (3/7/11 – 10/13/11)
Ramadan is Burnished Sunlight (part of This Light Slants Upward, published separately by The Ecstatic Exchange, 2011)
The Match That Becomes a Conflagration (10/14/11 – 5/9/12)
Down at the Deep End (5/10/12 –)

www.ingramcontent.com/pod-product-compliance
Lightning Source LLC
Chambersburg PA
CBHW020912090426
42736CB00008B/595